A Sensitive Heart

Vedanti Bhoyar

BookLeaf Publishing
India | USA | UK

Presentation by *BookLeaf Publishing*

Web: www.bookleafpub.com

E-mail: info@bookleafpub.com

ISBN: 9789358319200

First edition 2023

DEDICATION

For all those who live by their hearts…

ACKNOWLEDGEMENT

I acknowledge with great pleasure,

My Baba, Mummy and my sister, vishruti, who first encouraged me to put down my thoughts down on paper. I have to thank a special to my awesome husband Prasanna, From reading early drafts to giving me advice on my writings , he was as important to this book getting done as I was. Thank you so much, dear.

I am so grateful of "The BookLeaf Publishing team" for giving me this opportunity and publishing this book.

I would like to thank all the wonderful readers, who are free and sensitive souls and contributing kindness and love to the world.

Thank you to the Universe.

PREFACE

To the readers,

This book is all about the emotions, thoughts, motivation, healing and glimpse of everyday life. Every poem of this book is written in different timings of my life. I like to write about the beauty of sensitivity of heart , the way our heart see and feel the things so this book is consisting of feelings of my sensitive heart , towards the moment I felt should be noted down on paper. Few of these writings I wrote sitting in my balcony, few on late nights, few in parks and few during traveling. All of these are consisting of my tears and joy. "A Sensitive Heart" is for all of us who can feel, who   can fall and who want to live this life rather than been stuck in an emotional loop. The purpose of this book is to make everyone smile and allow their emotions to flow with these poems in their own way and make a safe space in their heart for themselves. This book is also my trying to make people understand and respect their sensitivity and heart. During my writing journey I was able to connect with myself and life a little more, hoping it will work the same for you too.
Vedanti

I Saw A Dream

I saw a dream,
Flying bird with
A new shade on its wings,

I saw a dream,
I saw a smile of my father and
A laughter of my mother,
The presence of my sister and
An aroma of the kitchen,

I saw the rain,
We get wet and
Ran towards few childhood friends,

I saw a summer with an ice cream
And winter with cozy evenings,

I saw my maa reading me a book,
I saw my dad getting me ready for school,

I saw my sister's cute smile
For a chocolate we used to buy,

I saw a dream,
Flying bird with,
A new shade on its wing,

I saw a night with music,
And a glass of wine,
Full moon and a passing time,

I saw a smile of my father
And a laughter of my mother,
The presence of my sister
And aroma of kitchen,

I saw a cartoon with my sister
And a home play for a future,
The books, the pencil, colours and stickers,

I saw the talks with my dad,
And a lunch with my mother,
The study with my sister and a picnic near the
hills,

I saw the birthdays,
I saw the innocence,
I saw the trains towards the temple and mosque,
I saw my sister's hand on mine for a long walk,

I saw a moment,
A memory and a life.
I saw the change to survive,

Replacing laughs with tears of Joy,
Books and pencil with Pen and mobile,
A cartoon with a movie and
Replacing a home play with life,

This new shades on wings gives the meaning to
life,
The new shade is where it could have broken or
die

I saw a dream,
Flying bird with,
A new shade on its Wing

The shade of change,
Courage and lovely being,
The shade of love,
Life and everything,
The shade of happiness,
Betterment and the new beginning,

I saw a dream,
Flying bird with,
A new shade on its wing....

A Courage Of Hope

Hope and courage, everyone says,
When nothing else exists, hope stays.

On the unfamiliar paths of life we tread,
Hope is what keeps us moving ahead.

When the paths diverge, and we anticipate
reunion,
If it doesn't happen, we hold onto hope's
communion.
Hoping to meet once more, we persist,
With the hope of keeping hope on our list.

If courage falters, what's the use of hope?
They seem intertwined, it's difficult to elope.

Those moments when we shatter and break,
Hope in the divine we embrace, for our sake.
Those moments when we stumble and fall,
Hope for the strength to rise, we call.

Is there a difference between hope and courage,
pray?
Having the 'courage to hope' is what they
convey.

The courage to keep hope alive is a unique endeavour,
It keeps the world going, forever and ever.

Holding onto hope might seem easy and light,
But is having the courage equally bright?

Hope's courage is the mightiest, they say,
It keeps us alive, lights our way each day.

It fuels our battles with the promise of success,
And the courage to win the next, no less.

Life, perhaps, is named after courage, I presume,
In which hope is carried as an heirloom.

Congratulations to those who are hopeful and brave,
To those who never let their hope wane.

Their duty is to share and expand this grace,
The hope for humanity's better embrace.

Hope for human transformation is grand,
Perhaps the greatest hope in this land.
But is it possible, you may inquire,
Through courage, we can certainly aspire.

The Hands Of My Dad

On a billing counter,
When he pays,
He don't buy the things,
But our happiness,
The hands of my dad,
Reveals the amount he paid,

From my first step of walk,
Till my first book from shop,
From playing with me, .till teaching me
The amount of time he spent,
The hands of my dad,
Reveals the time he paid,

From my first day in school,
Till I graduated from college,
The tears of joy of my achievements,
Till the sorrow of my see off,
The amount of emotions he faced,
The hands of my dad,
Reveals the emotions he paid,

From teaching me a bicycle, till letting me drive,
From letting me fall, till I reach the height,
The amount of strength he gave,

The hands my of dad,
Reveals the strength he paid,

From leaving me at hostel,
Till Letting me explore the world,
From letting me take my own decisions,
Till helping me in every situation,
The amount of courage I get,
The hands of my dad,
Reveals the courage he paid,

A young man,
Comes to see the world,
Have given the crown of responsibilities,
But he never gave up on possibilities,

He beings the journey of becoming a Father
This journey is somehow left unseen,
It's mandatory to make it seen,
It shows the journey of every young man,
The Amount of life they spent,
The hands of my dad,
Reveals the journey they paid,

How can I repay him?
Should it be only the monetary term or,
It should be in time, strength, courage and
emotions?

The hands of my dad.
Looks for my hand on theirs,
And this will be the payment made by us for
forever.

From my first existence, to my life's every
moment,
The hands of dad,
Reveals,
Everything,

He paid…

Imperfect Says I'm Perfect

A hesitation on stage,
Or a feeling of cage,
Struggle in communication,
Or a fear of separation,
Let it be, it's okay to have that,
As Imperfect says I'm perfect,

A crowded mind every morning,
OR sometimes your heart gives you some
warnings,
The sweat on a palms and body becomes river,
Or be it any indefinite fear,
Let it be, it's okay to have that,
As Imperfect says I'm perfect,

When you sense a fright to avoid your social
life,
And tell your friends a lot of lies,
When we switch off our phones to keep us hide,
Days with a dark room, low music and wine,
Or some days we just don't want to shine,
Let it be, it's okay to do that,
As Imperfect says I 'm perfect,

A fast ride on motorbike with no helmet on,
Heading towards a journey which is going to be
so long,
When nobody can stop you,
Not even your own mind,
Let it be, it's okay to do that,
As Imperfect says I 'm perfect,

A sudden leave from office,
A bunk from college,
Or just a sunny Tuesday noon,
At home on your bed,
When we start reading something,
Which we have already read,
Let it be, it's okay to do that,
As Imperfect says I'm perfect,

An impulse to put something on desired place,
Or washing your hands to keep it clean always,
Even if you know the world will not embrace,
Let it be, it's okay to do have that,
As Imperfect says I'm imperfect,

On these moments,
What we do,
Few of the things,
We can't undo,
Yet these endure keeps us alive,
In those instants where we can't survive,

World see these deeds as fatal flaws,
Even so,
It gives us some odds,
To think, rethink and
Unlock a treasure,
Succeeding ahead to give us real pleasure,

When at last a peace calls within,
We create our own song and starts to sing,
With an imperfect music,
And an imperfect notes,
Still we proceed, and make it our goal,
Let it be and it's okay to do that,
As Imperfect says I 'm perfect,

Perfection,
Imperfection is a myth enough,
Stick with your heart,
After all the world is tough,

At times we want to perceive the pain,
When we are healed and,
Still want to heal again,
Let it be, it's okay to accept that,
As Imperfect says,
I 'm,

Perfect.

An Indo-Western Naari

It started with the day she was born,
Beautiful she with beautiful heart,
But unknown about the world's wars,
Innocently playing with fairy dolls,
Thinking she is the one too,
Playing with the toy house,
Thinking she belongs there too,

Days and years passed,
The doll got fade,
The toy house got lost,
It started with the day she took her first breath,
A heart so pure untouched by hate,

Days and years relentlessly passed,
The World demands and give her a task,
Task to get her marry,
But also want to count her salary,

Now she is a doll with one hand holding 'Ghar
-Sansar',
The other with lappy and car,
She belongs to the toy house where,
She is playing with her dreams,
Stuck between reality and memes,

Days and years passed,
Now the food, air, and people nothing is ideal,
But society ask for, her ideal cycles,
Her heart is divided, it's plain to see,
Responsibility, dreams and love all three,

From morning till night,
She is fighting the same fight,
Even if one shoulder falters sometimes,
World quickly forget her plight,
She yearns for rest,
To see the light,

From saree to suit,
Leggings till jeans,
From outfit till life,
She is trying to be alive,
In journey of life,
She struggles to survive,
Let s celebrate her strength,
Let her truly thrive,
Call her 'Shakti ' only, not 'Bichari',
You see,
This is the tale of ,
An Indo-western Naari.

Memories-A Non-closing Door

"Memories" are connected with us before our
birth,
We were inside the womb,
But still wanted to get heard,
"Memories -A non-closing door",
When it opens,
Ocean start flowing,
Full of emotions,

Memory of first step
And first birthday cake,
The nostalgic crowd and long school break,
We close our eyes and live that again,
Memories -a non-closing door,
Always keeps us awake,

The moment freezes,
And gives us goose bumps,
Sometimes we don't know,
How to deal with it and
We get ourselves drunk,
Memories of first proposal,
Till it closed away,

A non-closing door,
Opens all the way.

An afternoon in summer,
With cartoon and cooler,
Eating ice candy full of colours,
Just living in the moment,
Without any fear,
In our heart such memories are there,

Cozy wind of winter and raining drops of water,
Hot soup in lunch and dinner by mother,
Feeling entirely the weather,
To sense the life together,
To this non closing door of memories
We have to surrender,

Days when we got confused,
And follow the different route,
Roaming on road,
With an ugly look,
Memories of those
Haunting phase,
Sometimes we want to reboot,
With this non closing door of memories,
We want to heal our wounds,

Memory of first love, and the first date,
Memories of those one, we used to hate,
Some we remember, some get forget, but
Those are there always,
Just need some break
Once it get triggered,
It hurts so bad,
For someone else it may feel great,
Few feel afraid
Few celebrate,
From this non closing door,
No one can escape,

How memories create, we all know by
ourselves,
This moment is converting in memory itself,
Let's live every moment in its fullest,
But how to do it,
Not anyone tells,

Well it's an art to create a memory you want,
See that moment in life and hold it in your hand,
See it,
Sense it, and
Breathe it twice,
You should be aware of your every insight,

Door of memory is open,
To let everything pass,
So we can't hold the moments,
It's our biggest loss,

But once we get control over every moment,
We feel it wholly and
Never regret,
In such way only good memories remains,
And non-closing door of memory -
Never gives us pain

We have the power to,
To make it and renewed,
When we want to give tribute,
In this journey everyone contributes,
And
A non-closing door of memory,
Still,
Continued...

A Bowl Of Rice

A bowl of rice,
Full of love and care,

When in the chilly mornings of winter,
My mother prepares spinach and bread,
She also gives me a bowl of rice,
Full of hard work and grace.

Whether it's a missing button from my
childhood,
Or a bindi from my youth,
The book of stories,
Or the world of music,
From childhood till now,
She is always there, and
I have always received
A bowl of rice
Full of love and care.

Putting mango pickle in jars during summers,
Asking her for some coins to buy ice creams of
different flavours,
Teaching me the little things in life,
Wiping my tearful eyes,
In all of this, she never fail to share,

A bowl of rice,
Full of love and care.

Making two braids for my sister and me,
Doing homework after school, all of us three,
Becoming a child herself in our childhood,
Telling us how to be good,
In our life the place she bears,
And always make for us,
A bowl of rice,
Full of love and care.

Introducing me to my femininity,
Making me to understand every opportunity,
Keeping courage in my tears too,
Asking me to always be fair,
Yet giving me,
A bowl of rice,
Full of love and care.

When I break down in life,
She puts me back together,
When I need her the most, she stands for me
there,
She feels like a friend along with my mother,
With this she always remember,
A bowl of rice,
Full of love and care.

She fights with the world for me,
Adapts herself every moment,
Tolerates all my misbehaviours,
And forgives me within a second
But never forgets,
A bowl of rice,
Full of love and care.

Even after reading only few books,
She gives me the wisdom of life,
She lives every moment for us,
And always ready to adjust,
She Nurture us for nine months
In her womb,
Till we get completely groomed,
With her no one can compare.
And every day,
She feeds me with,
A bowl of rice,
Full of love and care.

What motherhood feels like?
Can it be expressed in words?
She is like God,
For all of us,
Leaving her dreams behind,
She spends her life for us,
And never forgets

A bowl of rice,
Full of love and care.

Your sacrifice knows no end,
There are no words like your emotions,
You run the entire world,
Yet, you become sad for some reason,
You are nature, you are power,
You are our glare,
And you make,
A bowl of rice,
Full of love and care.

Oh mother, how can we repay your debt?
How can we express our gratitude?
We can just wish
That we spend,
Our lives at your feet,
You stay with us every moment,
Smiling like this forever,
And always give us,
A bowl of rice,
Full of ,
Love and care.

My First Trust On You

My first trust on you is like,
The glow of a shining moon in the darkest night,

You are the life of my life,
And the breath of my breath,
The smile in my sorrows,
Which keeps me alive,
My first trust on you is like,
Like two stars entwined,

As if I've lived my entire life just to reach you,
As if every heartbeat has raced to meet you,
I don't know how many lifetimes destiny
explored,
I laughed, cried, wandered, but didn't halt,

Your gaze with those eyes,
And a touch so divine,
Crossing oceans to reach me,
And let our love shine.
My first trust on you is like,
The end of countless waiting of lifetimes',

Seeing you, and holding your hand to walk,
Having faith in you for every little talk,
Letting you become my life on my own,
The feelings of my heart are meant to shown,
That's all I always seek,
My first trust on you is like,
A pinch of colour on my cheek,

Your desire to save me from every trouble,
Your voice like the melody of a flute,
I forget all struggles,
Making my laughter blend into me,
My soul become light and free,
As time passes our love grows,
My first trust on you is like,
The fragrance of a rose,

Amidst all logics, and hurdles in the world,
You brought that feather so light and pearled,
Keeping aside your pain and hurt,
You choose my happiness instead
My first trust on you is like,
A sacred thread,

Watching time standstill, forgetting what we
know
Those Laughs with you, wherever we go,
Encouraging me in life,
For every highs and lows

My first trust on you is like,
The final union of two souls,

Your first two words, brighten my eyes,
Transformed every upcoming sunrise in my life,
My soul always says, you are the one
My first trust on you is like,
A ray of the sun,

Your hand in mine, we let ourselves heard,
Giving each other support, Fearless of the world
Living what we love,
Don't bother, who judge
My first trust in you is like,
The angelic touch,

I still live on this trust today, for a beautiful view
I just lower my eyes and raise them to see you,
You will always be my lifeline
My first trust on you is like,
The sweet smile of the divine

It was there before, it is there today,
And will remain always there, my love on you,
My life for you
And my first trust,
Only on you,

For forever.

The Sound Of Pause

When for a while our heart stops,
And our breath can't take any path,
We pause in a pain,
To listen the sound of pause,

When life get stuck at one place,
And there is no one to take care of ourselves,
We pause in a shock,
And listen the sound of pause,

When we sit alone with our notions,
To give them a correct motion,
We pause in one perception,
To listen the sound of pause,

When some loved one goes away,
And we miss their existence every single day,
We pause in their presence,
And listen the sound of pause,

When we hold a tiny child,
And look at their beautiful smile,
We pause in the beauty of God,
To listens the sound of pause,

When we hold someone's hand for forever,
And vow of never leaving it ever,
We pause in a moment, together,
And listen to the sound of pause,

When we complete our climb,
And hold the trophy for the first time,
We pause in the triumph,
To listen the sound of pause,

But sometimes we need an intension,
To express the experience,
And let the moment cherish inside our heart,
To listen the sound of pause,

When we take a step,
Towards the silence inside,
And seek something which will be always by
our side,
"We are the gift to ourselves" we realize,
To regard the pause in life,
When universe gives us a chance,
To grasp it and dance,
We pause in a glance,
To listen the sound of pause,

When sorrows of life don't have any cause,
We still saunter the road we came across,
And choose to be our own boss,
Let's give ourselves a big applause,
And listen,
The sound of,
Pause.

Today I am One Year Older Than You

I am at same place you used to be,
Watching a beautiful view,
I sense your presence,
Your beautiful smile,
It feels something new,
Today I am one year older than you,

You introduce me this place earlier,
Now I am living in this heaven
When I think about you,
Childhood memories gets freshen,

I miss you every day,
While making a morning tea,
Hoping you to see,
Then I realise suddenly,
.that you are not there anymore,
As God set you free,
Still around me I can see your hue,
Today I am one year older than you,

Those childhood plays,
Decorating home, and
Wearing different outfits,

Remembering we can't do it again,
Gives me glitz,
Couldn't you stayed, a little few?
Today I am 1 year older than you,

You were my friend, was like my sister,
Your beautiful smile and free laughter,
Always showed that you was never a quitter,
Knowing you left,
Makes me feel blue,
Today I am one year older than you,
,

Yes today is my birthday,
And I wish you could have stayed,
Those nostalgic celebrations with you and a
piece of cake,
Today, all seems fade,
It feels like yesterday,
When we were saying a goodbye at evening,
Never thought it will be our last meeting,

Ruchi, A symbol of my early life,
I respect your sacrifice,
And I want you back, at any price,
Hope we cd take birth twice,
And there will be no any due,
Today I am one year older than you,

Life is still going on. ,.
But In our girlhood nobody won,
The bond with my innocence is ruined,
As you are gone,
Every day I recall your virtues,
And today I am one year older than you

Days will pass,
And at last,
I will wait the day,
We will again come across,

And that day I will rescue you,

Today, I am one year older than you,

Whisper of The Universe

In the realm where stars entwine and galaxies
bestow,
The Universe, a silent guide, in its vastness we
do know.
Is it God, a deity, or perhaps, no entity at all?
Does it truly matter, as we heed its cosmic call?

In worship of God, belief in deities, love for
humanity's grace,
Acceptance of our inner selves, all intertwined
in one embrace.
These feelings lead us down a path, to become a
true believer,
Even in the belief of "nothing," it's a faith that
can't deceive us.

For believing in "nothing" is a belief in
something profound,
In the beauty of worship and in humanity's
grace, we're bound.
The Universe whispers softly, "I allow," in its
cosmic dance,
As we make our choices in this existence, we
have a chance.

Choose your God, your deity, your humanity,
and yourself,
Or choose no one at all, let your inner wisdom
delve.
The Universe watches, saying, "I allow" to our
choices wide,
Hate, revenge, sorrow, and grief, or the love
that's bona fide.

But choose wisely, for in these choices,
something's key,
The wellness of ourselves and others, the path to
harmony.
The Universe grants us everything if we choose
with care,
Becoming one with its cosmic flow, a journey
we all share.

Yet if we falter in our choices, lost in the quest
for the one,
The Universe still whispers, "I allow," until the
search is done.
"I allow you, you are mine, and I am yours," it
softly sings,
In this cosmic symphony, we're all connected by
its strings.

Choose to heal, choose to bleed, accept, and
expect,
Choose to live, choose to die, with each choice,
we connect.
The Universe, with gentle wisdom, echoes its
decree,
"I allow," it says, as we shape our destiny, wild
and free.

In the tapestry of life we weave, it listens to our
plea,
As we act, think, and ponder, the Universe's
mystery.
It keeps our destiny updating, in a dance so
grand,
As we choose our path, our karma, in this
cosmic land.

So choose your destiny, embrace your karma's
sway,
Choose to stay and evolve, let the Universe
guide your way.
In the grand design of existence, the Universe
stands tall,
Whispering softly, "I allow," as we journey
through it all.

Sibling - A Saviour

The day they get born,
Our life transforms,
Somewhere from the angels,
We got the gift so warm,

They grew up with us sharing the life,
We have been always each other's guide,
Time spent with them, memories and joys,
Are unable to describe,
Sibling - A Saviour,
Are Always by our side,

Some like mom, some like dad,
Both of us are always attached,
But sometimes we fight and crash,
On 'Who have been picked up from the trash?'

From childhoods monkey tricks,
And an unplanned trips,
From hitting a goal or last ball's six,
And dancing on remix,
From a lot of conflicts
Till letting it get fixed
Sibling-A Saviour,
Are Always in our list,

A sister or a brother,
Does it really matter? ,
They fond of one another and,
Know each other better
Sibling - a Saviour,
Discovers the life together,

But their lovely connection is not merely,
Life look at them so clearly,
Earning same values from their parents,
They pledge to follow it so sincerely,
Sibling - A Saviour,
Such bond is found so rarely,

A saviour is the one who keep us safe and alive,
Siblings are, like precious gem of our eyes,
When life goes on and we keep survive,
They come in life, when no one arrives,
Sibling - A saviour,
Keeps us revive,

From first day of living,
Till the last breath,
We love our parents,
And want them again and again,
They are the saviour of our life,
In sibling, a part of them is always alive,
Sibling- a saviour

Walks with us thousand miles,
With a smile,
Helps us to thrive,

From lullabies,
Till sacrifice,

Sibling - a saviour,
Will always,
Make our life,
A beautiful paradise.......

The Unexpected

The life should be this,
We expect, when it goes wrong, we reject,
But,
When it goes even what we want,
Still there is a vacuum inside our heart which
haunts,
And At this point,
The unexpected things goes along,

Suddenly we got one chance,
At sudden someone comes to warn,
Suddenly we get helping hand,
Or at sudden we fall at some place,
All these comes when we don't expect,
But lead us in way we prayed,
All of these things give us a grant,
When the unexpected things, comes along,

Is unexpected always wrong?
Or sometimes we expect the small,
Once I dreamed for a flower,
And I got the bouquet to empower,
Full of rose, lilies, and sunflower,
And I got a full garden till dawn,
Because the unexpected things, goes along,

Do unexpected always hurt?
Or sometimes we are not ready to convert?
Once I expected to be at first,
But somewhere I lost in desert,
I came at last but hit the flag,
Everyone was happy,
But I was sad,
I completed the journey and came out strong,
Because the unexpected things, goes along

Is unexpected thing always good?
Or sometimes it destroys our mood,
Once I asked God for one task,
But nothing happened, not even anyone asked,
It broke my heart like
Broken glass,
And killed me from inside,
Like I am never going to pass,
But it gave me the lesson I want,
I grew up like, I got reborn,
All these happens
Because the unexpected things, goes along,

Don't bother, don't fear,
At last it's all okay my dear,
We block our expectations,
To live and cheer, But
What if we expect the unexpected near?

To see the beauty of life and sing a song,
Because the unexpected things, goes along

So let's feel free and light,
And expect the things but with insight,
To stop our sorrows be prolong,
Because the unexpected things, Goes along,

It may hurt,
It may wrong,
It may break you so strong,
But the reason have reason,
To place you where you belong, and
Let the unexpected things,
Goes along…

I Wish

I wish that together we could make the
incomplete dream complete,
I wish I could get forgiveness like you, and
another chance to meet
Our love is lost, I don't know where, our
happiness is gone,

I wish the wind comes again carrying the same
memories,
I wish my heart tells me to keep beating and not
to get freeze,
Our warmth is lost, I don't know where, our
affection is gone,

I wish that garden calls again and says come for
a while,
I wish that flower blooms again and says
happiness with a smile,
Our joy is lost, I don't know where, our
connection is gone,

I wish I could see old us again,
I wish you were still my love, hope we could
regain,
I wish I could visit the old places with you,

And sing our favourites,
Our grace is lost, I don't where, our faith is gone

I wish these memories were not only memories,
I wish they were true,

I wish I could be all yours,
And I could get just a little of you.....

The Pace Of Life

We need to understand,
We need to realize,
The love of our loved ones and
The pace of life...

We must realize that "age" is more important,
Than the mistakes made at any age,
What we learn from our mistakes is even more
valuable than,
The mistakes themselves.

Sometimes we need to realize that,
'The person' who is on the wrong path,
Who is making mistakes?
Is more important than the mistakes he is
making,

We need to understand that,
the most important thing in life is "life" itself,
We need to know,
We need to realize,
The love of our loved ones and
The pace of life...

We must understand that,
We should not settle for,
Anything less than the best in our search for a
better life.

We need to understand that in that moment,
"The moment" is more important than "right and
wrong,"

We need to know...
Happiness is more important than sorrow,
That we deserve to be happy,
That we have the right to be happy.

Sometimes it is important to realize that,
The things we say "sometimes" are never
important at any time,
It is important to understand that conversation is
essential along the way,
It is important to understand that love is
necessary,
It is also important to understand that until love
reaches worship, it remains incomplete,

We need to know,
We need to realize,
The love of our loved ones and
The pace of life...

We need to understand that,
Whether there is a God or not,
Love and humanity is,

We need to understand that,
There is no need for a specific face, person or
permission for worship,

We need to understand that whether it's a
journey or,
The first step of a journey,
'It is' more important than anything else,
anytime, anywhere, 'it is' important.

We need to know,
We need to realize,
The love of our loved ones and
The pace of life...

It is important to understand that,
Every moment counts as a memory and,
Every memory has its value,
And that value depends on the individual,

We need to understand that,
Someone is already writing our story,
Or we are writing it ourselves,

The book has long been open...

Our ink, our style, our pages, and our way...

We need to feel that people are still reading
books of life,
For everyone, every day, every moment,

It is important to understand,
How do we evaluate our book based on its first
pages or its last pages?
What do we write when we know the final page?

If the final page is known, what do you write?
Respect?
Intention?
Work?
Knowing?
Right?
Wrong?
Worship?
Or love?

We need to understand that,
Kindness is the only right,
And aggression is the only wrong.

There is a need to understand and promote that...
For kindness, no specific occasion, person, or
place is needed,
Only a true human heart is needed,

We need to know,
We need to realize,
The love of our loved ones and
The pace of life...

We need to understand that,
For a moment, just for a moment, there is only
one life...
Feeling the voice of your breath.
Desiring the best.
The love of our loved ones and the pace of life...

It is important to understand...
Every day,
Every moment... is a life.
There is a need to write,
Your own words in your book.

Every moment, we need to succeed...
To feel it,
To know it.

We need to know,
We need to feel,
The love of our loved ones and
The pace of life...

When You are There

Every moment is flowing with the direction of
the wind,
There is no count of these moments,
It always slips from our eyes
However there is a lot of pain in life,
But when you are there,
I do not realize,

One path, one place, one time, one reason,
One pain somewhere in a space of heart hidden,
No one has any strength in these moments,
Nobody can refuse when it arise,
However there is so much pain in life,
But when you are there, I don't realize,

Plant from a seed,
Bud from a plant,
Flower from a bud,
And life is like a flower in mud,
But not every flower has the same colour on,
And it is not any disguise
However there is so much pain in life,
But when you are there,
I don't realize,

If you are there then words are lyrics,
If you are there then Voice is music,
If you are there my life is life,
Not everyone is like you,
Pure and wise,
However there is a lot of pain in life,
But when you are there,
I don't realize,

Who makes your life,
A beautiful surprise,
This you is "me"
I recognise,
However there is a lot of pain in life,
But if I am there with myself,

I don't realize.

One Goodbye

Sometimes it hurts like a thorn,
That continues ache of heart is heavy,
One goodbye to this pain of hurt,

Sometimes it makes us feel guilty like a rotten
water,
That makes us stop for forever, one
 Goodbye to these tears of guilt,

Sometimes it kills our confidence like a broken
glass,
That keep us under a delusion,
One goodbye to this useless illusion,

Sometimes there is a lot of fear like a knife near
the neck,
That make our every sec like a hell,
One goodbye to this scary feel,

Sometimes it is so lonely like a dark cave,
That pierce our heart with complete silence,
One goodbye to this alone noise.

Sometimes it is so hopeless like a trash in bin,
That keeps us as low as possible until it win,
One goodbye to this worthless thing,

Sometimes it is so empty like an uncropped
land,
That keeps us desiring for a pond
A goodbye to this
Sad hope

Never bother to ask yourself what is it?
Which makes us hurt, hopeless, empty and
lonely within?

Sometimes questioning our feelings,
Gives us answers,
Which may never get solved by any masters,

One goodbye to lonely nights,
One goodbye to tearful vibes,
One goodbye to that
Emptiness,
One goodbye to that pain,

Be brave to feel yourself,
Be brave to fall yourself,
Be brave to get up again,

And
Be brave to ask for help,

Sometimes some unknown keeps you there,
Like you know that miracle needed somewhere,
Let's say,
A BIG Goodbye to all that is not require.

Who is Really There For You

Who is really there for you?
Those who like your posts daily,
Or those who knows when you are happy, sad or
lonely,
When we sit together, and still look for someone
on internet,
We think we are connecting, but can't even talk,
without a cigarette,
Whom we are fooling,
What is exactly true?
Just sit and think once,
Who is really there for you?

When we are kid,
We play and think,
Our toys and friends are the sweetest thing,
Forever they will be there with us,
Playing around and running behind the pups,
But time at sudden take a spins,
To show a different venue,
Just sit and think once,
Who is really there for you?

Somewhere ahead,
Some new people come,
We study, we grow,
We explore the world,
Some stick for a long,
Few get stuck,
We think this time they are going to be with us,
But what is coming ahead no one knew,
Just sit and think once,
Who is really there for you?

Family stands always with us,
Until we grow as an adult,
They give us support, love and care,
Fill us with the faith,
They are there, will be always,
But gradually this bond changes,
Some hides, some lies, make this bond renew,
Just sit and think once,
Who is really there for you??

At 30s one come to become a soulmate,
Later we realise it's just a part of life everyone
should get,
When one get sick, other helps,
It gives us strength but can't take our pain,

We juggle in time with bitter and sweet
memories,
And in between we find,
There is a need to meet,
The one is really strong,
The one who don't needs any arm,
One who live without fear,
One who finds oneself near,
Who is that one? Take a quick view,
Just sit and think once, .who is really there for
you?

When old friends get vanished, we look for new
ones
At this time unexpected appears,
When life turns more,
A new chapter arrives,
Not all are gone,
But few remains
In the name of responsibilities and
commitments,
Till last breath they stick like a glue,
So just sit and think once,
Who is really there for you?

If we stop somewhere,
We seek someone to hold,
We run here and there,
But everyone scolds,

At this time,
Our own hands are helping hands,
No one comes,
Nobody take a chance,
We think we won,
But this loop goes on,
Maybe somewhere we missed the clue,
So just sit and think once,
Who is really there for you?

Old age arrives,
We followed all rules,
To not to die alone and free our soul,
Still somewhere in heart,
A whole speaks,
Who are you?
What did you do to yourself?
What you had unique?

We get shocked with huge confusion,
I followed what they said,
Still I am a looser?

The loud voice talks,
Where were you lost?
This is a different path,
You could have earn all the cards,
You sold yourself, for everyone you knew,
Thinking they will be there to help you,

If you could have listen to your intuition,
Life must have gave you a different mission,
In this last phase of life,
Vast questions comes,
But the one needs review,
Is,

Who was really there for you?

Oh! Nature

Oh! Nature,
River, mountain, forest and glacier,
You are our precursor,
We have been always a learners,

Oh! Nature,
Teach us the patience of a seed,
Help us to precise our deeds,
Bless us with the awareness of life's course,
Help us to learn it and decode,

Grant us the beauty of the wild,
Teach us how to always be styled,
Bless us with the melody of water,
Help us to save our laughter,
Oh nature,
Instil us how to be better

Bless us with togetherness,
And teach us how to reduce hate,
Grant us the silence of night,
Teach us how to shine bright
Guide us with the dim of the seasons,
Help us to know the reasons,

Sometimes teach us how to be loud,
To save the things around,
Oh! Nature,
You are so profound,

Teach me the peace like a flowing river and
clear sky,
And how to keep our soul glorify,
Bless us with courage of standing alone like a
mountain,
Bless us with the power like a tree, how it
stands,
Oh ! Nature,
How to be like you, so grand,

Bless us with trust to reach at the top,
Bless us with the route
Which teaches us a lot,
Oh nature,
Be with us till last,

To spoil you, we are so sorry,
It must be thing we all should worry,
We ruin you every day,
Still you bless us in all the way,

You are around us,
Not less a than any miracle,
We are you,

Soil, air and water,
You are like a mother,
Who nurtures us,
And also a divine,
Who teaches us,

When we forgot your touch,
Like a child has lost his mother
We get sick,
And everything vanished in just one blink. ,

You are the power,
You are supreme,

Oh, lovely nature,
Teach us the balance,
Teach us a sync,
And,
Bless us with insight,
That,

You are within….

Story Behind The Story

Heartbeat stops, moisture in eyes,
Fighting against the inside war,
The story behind the story is much more,

There are lips but no speech,
There is speech but no sound,
There is sound but no voice,
There is voice but no situation,
Why life feels so poor,
The story behind the story is much more,

It have spoken,
It have seen,
It have written,
It have read,
It is filled with sorrows, love, affection and
expression,
Each have a different core,
Because,
The story behind the story is ,
Much more....

I Bow Down

I bow down,
To my breath,
My blink and my beat,
For being there,
And letting my days repeat,

To my body,
For giving me sense,
To feel, fight and
Make me seen,

I bow down,
Towards my happiness,
For all those beautiful moments,
I lived and keep living,

To my loved ones,
Who makes my life brightest as the sun,

I bow down,
To the pain
Which makes me stronger
 Gives me strength and makes me wise,

My soul,
And to my intuition,
For keeping me always hopeful and alive,

I bow down
To my teachers,
Who taught me the life, and
Give us light

To the ones,
Who came and left,
Teaching me something
So important to get,

I bow down
To the surprises in life,
Which made me believe in miracle,
That I can't forget,

I bow down to my past,
And present,
For creating a better future,

To those days,
Which taught me grace,
Thanks to a beautiful culture,
I bow down,
To the sorrows,

Which grant me hope,
To the tears,
For teaching me how to cope,

I bow down to,
My life,
I bow down,
To wear a crown,
In regards
This Far,

How I survived...

www.ingramcontent.com/pod-product-compliance
Lightning Source LLC
LaVergne TN
LVHW021228200726